BLUE MANOR PHONICS

Learning to Read the **easy** *way!*

Britton LaTulippe

Introduction

There are three primary features that set Blue Manor's phonics system apart from the others: 5-Minute Lessons, No Pictures, and Simplicity.

5-Minute Lessons: It is virtually impossible to stop a child from learning that which he desires to learn, and equally impossible to teach a child what he does not desire to learn. Since this book is for beginners, it is likely to leave a first and lasting impression on your children about reading.

If the lessons are long and painful, overwhelming and tedious, your child will develop a negative opinion of reading. He will imagine lessons are hard because he is no good at it, and the harder you push, the more he will resist.

Blue Manor has solved this dilemma by creating 5-Minute Lessons. It is not a law, but a general rule, that young children (3 to 5 years old) learn the best when the lessons are short and sweet. We have found that for most children in this age range, 5 minutes is the sweet spot. They could go longer, but it is best to end on a high, rather than just fizzling out.

Since children using our program range in age and ability, some children will need a little more time and others a little less for each lesson, but we recommend keeping it as close to the 5-minute mark as possible. If a lesson begins to exceed 5 minutes, consider saving the rest for the next lesson. It is normal, especially in the beginning, to repeat the same lesson several times before children fully master it.

Before introducing a new lesson, take a minute and review the previous content. If you have forgotten the last lesson, make that your lesson of the day. There is no need to rush the process - slow and steady wins the race. Build a strong foundation in the beginning and your children will fly through the later lessons.

If you want to move through the lessons faster, you might try three 5-minute lessons a day, one before each meal, perhaps.

No Pictures: It probably seems strange to call the lack of something a feature. However, you will find that by intentionally excluding pictures from our phonics curriculum, your job of teaching is made easier and more effective.

When is it comes to learning how to read, pictures often serve as an insurmountable barrier, and at the very least, an unnecessary crutch. A child doesn't have to "read" apple when the apple is pictured next to the word. Children who learn to read with images will often look to the pictures first, and then turn back the words and try to make sense of them.

However, pictures are fun to look at. That is why we have included silly pictures in our early readers. There are early readers for both Level 1 and Level 2. After his lesson, reward your child with a fun reading in his favorite Blue Manor early reader.

Simplicity: Simplicity is important for both the teacher and the student. You should not need a teaching degree in order to teach a young child how to read. And complex systems will only frustrate your child.

That is why this book is designed to be overly simple. Each lesson is only 5 minutes, and even that is broken into smaller baby steps. You won't need to add anything, or plan anything – we have done all that for you. So, don't overthink this. Trust the system. Follow it lesson by and lesson, and you will be amazed at its effectiveness.

Early Readers: If you do not already have Blue Manor's Phonics Early Readers, I would highly recommend them. They are broken into two sets: Level 1 and Level 2. The fun stories are uniquely written with words that correspond to the appropriate reading level. For instance, once your child can read everything in Level 1, he should be able to read every word in the Level 1 early readers. And there is even an early reader that your child should be able to handle after just a handful of Level 1 lessons!

Nothing can be more frustrating to children as they learn to read than not finding books to match their reading level. The best way to match their reading level is to use our early readers.

We have not included early readers for Level 3 because once your child completes Level 3, he should be able to read most children's books and even some chapter books.

Additional Resources: This book is certainly a standalone phonics system. You don't need anything else to teach your child to read. Still, there are additional resources that you will find helpful.

Blue Manor offers a FREE Home Education book that you can download from www.BlueManorEducation.com. Our Home Education book describes the "Manor Way," plus is loaded with tons of great teaching tips and insights that will help you teach like a pro!

We also offer a digital version of our phonics system. It is great because the lessons and early readers include audio, giving children the power to teach themselves how to read!

Thank you for choosing Blue Manor to assist you! You are going to be great, and more importantly, your kids are going to excel!

Happy teaching,
Britton LaTulippe

Level 1

Level 1 Phonics Reading is designed to teach your children to read, or at least begin the process. We do not cover all the sound combinations in Level 1, but by the time your little ones have completed this level, they will understand the concept of combining letters to make sounds and combining sounds to make words.

The great thing about this method is that your children will learn to read a word in their very first phonics lesson. The letter U is natural and easy to pronounce, especially for young children. That is why we start with the letter U. Then we add the letter P. P is also easy to say. Next you have your children combine the two sounds and read UP. In just a few minutes they have learned to read their first word.

We do not recommend that you add to the material in this book. To prevent any confusion, we have limited the material on each page to only the most essential and relevant. Thus, we recommend that you limit your descriptions to the few sentences at the bottom of each page, and do not to add more words until they have mastered these. The material in parentheses will help you pronounce the sounds correctly so you don't confuse your child.

As your children become familiar with the words,

they may be tempted to guess, or they may automatically recognize the words by sight. Do not allow them to "sight read." At this stage, you should have them sound out each letter and then combine the sounds into one word.

Have them use their finger to follow each letter, left to right, as they say each letter sound. Then, in a sweeping motion, blend the sounds to make a word. This will help your children hear the different sound combinations and establish the habit of reading from left to right. If they are having trouble blending or hearing the sounds that make the word, break up the word into smaller parts. Have them blend two letter sounds together and then add the last sound.

Because of the constant repetition of the words, your children will eventually have the words memorized, but still you must have them sound each word out individually or they might develop the habit of guessing, even after you start introducing new words. Of course, once they have fully mastered the concept of reading, it is OK to sight-read. After all, when is the last time that you as an adult sounded out a word? Adults rarely have to sound out words because we have such a large variety of memorized words. So, sight reading is not always bad – it is just unproductive at this early stage of learning.

Once your children can easily sound out the letters and letter combinations, they are ready to move on to the next phonics level.

A B C D E F G H I J
K L M N O P Q R S
T U V W X Y Z

These are letters. There are *26* different letters in our alphabet.

Aa   Aa. This is the letter A.
Big A and little a.

Bb   Bb. This is the letter B.
Big B and little b.

Cc Cc. This is the letter C.
Big C and little c.

Lesson 2

Dd Dd. This is the letter D.
Big D and little d.

Ee Ee. This is the letter E.
Big E and little e.

Ff Ff. This is the letter F.
Big F and little f.

Gg Gg. This is the letter G.
Big G and little g.

Lesson 3

Hh — Hh. This is the letter H. Big H and little h.

Ii — Ii. This is the letter I. Big I and little i.

Jj — Jj. This is the letter J. Big J and little j.

Kk — Kk. This is the letter K. Big K and little k.

Ll — Ll. This is the letter L. Big L and little l.

11

Lesson 4

Mm   Mm. This is the letter M. Big M and little m.

Nn   Nn. This is the letter N. Big N and little n.

Oo   Oo. This is the letter O. Big O and little o.

Pp   Pp. This is the letter P. Big P and little p.

Qq   Qq. This is the letter Q. Big Q and little q.

Lesson 5

Rr   Rr. This is the letter R.
Big R and little r.

Ss   Ss. This is the letter S.
Big S and little s.

Tt   Tt. This is the letter T.
Big T and little t.

Uu   Uu. This is the letter U.
Big U and little u.

Vv   Vv. This is the letter V.
Big V and little v.

Lesson 6

Ww Ww. This is the letter W. Big W and little w.

Xx Xx. This is the letter X. Big X and little x.

Yy Yy. This is the letter Y. Big Y and little y.

Zz Zz. This is the letter Z. Big Z and little z.

Lesson 7

ZSMBUORKGQVDY
CEHXNJALIFPTW

**Starting with "A" and ending with "Z,"
find all the capital letters of the alphabet.**

gkosdneqcibrju
fypmtwzlhvxa

**Starting with "a" and ending with "z," find
all the lowercase letters of the alphabet.**

Lesson 8 (Phonics)

U   This is the letter U. U says "uh," like uh-uh-umbrella.

P   This is the letter P. P says "P," like p-p-puppy.

UP   uh-P. UP. Can you point up?

Note: Sound the letters out separately. Then blend them together.

PUP   P-uh-P. PUP. A PUP is a baby dog.

C   This is the letter C. C says "C," like c-c-cat.

CUP   C-uh-P. CUP. You drink from a CUP.

A   This is the letter A. A says "A," like a-a-apple.

CAP   C-A-P. CAP. A CAP is a small hat or the lid on a bottle.

Lesson 10

T   This is the letter T. T says "T," like t-t-turtle.

AT   A-T. AT. We are AT the store.

PAT   P-A-T. PAT. Can you PAT your head?

TAP   T-A-P. TAP. TAP your finger on the table.

CUT   C-uh-T. CUT. We use scissors to CUT paper.

CAT C-A-T. CAT. That CAT is chasing a mouse.

Lesson 11

H This is the letter H. H says "H," like h-h-hat.

HAT H-A-T. HAT. Do you wear a HAT on your head?

O This is the letter O. O says "awe" like o-o-octopus.

HOP H-awe-P. HOP. The frog loves to HOP.

19

HOT H-awe-T. HOT. Fire is very HOT.

POP P-awe-P. POP. I don't want to POP my balloon.

POT P-awe-T. POT. The chef cooks food in a POT.

COP C-awe-P. COP. A policeman is called a COP.

TOP T-awe-P. TOP. Can you touch the TOP of your head?

COT C-awe-T. COT. A COT is a small bed.

Lesson 12

G   This is the letter G. G says "G" like g-g-great.

GAG   G-A-G. GAG. Don't choke and GAG on your food.

HUG   H-uh-G. HUG. Will you please give me a HUG?

GOT   G-awe-T. GOT. I GOT a new game for Christmas.

GAP   G-A-P. GAP. A GAP is a space between two objects.

HOG H-awe-G. HOG. A HOG is a big pig.

TAG T-A-G. TAG. Where is the price TAG?

TUG T-uh-G. TUG. Can you TUG on your shirt?

Lesson 13

B This is the letter B. B says "B," like b-b-ball.

BOB B-awe-B. BOB. Can you BOB your head up and down?

BUG B-uh-G. BUG. That BUG is crawling away.

BAT B-A-T. BAT. Hit the ball with the BAT.

BAG B-A-G. BAG. I put the groceries in a BAG.

CUB C-uh-B. CUB. A baby bear is called a CUB.

BUT B-uh-T. BUT. I want to play, BUT I have to go to bed.

COB C-awe-B. COB. I love corn on the COB!

TUB T-uh-B. TUB. I take a bath in a TUB.

Lesson 14

I This is the letter I. I says "ih" like i-i-insect.

IT I-T. IT. The dog ate IT!

HIT H-I-T. HIT. Do not HIT other people.

BIB B-I-B. BIB. Do you wear a BIB when you eat?

BIG   B-I-G. BIG. The lion is very BIG.

BIT   B-I-T. BIT. My hamster BIT me!

PIG   P-I-G. PIG. Don't eat like a PIG.

TIP   T-I-P. TIP. Did you TIP your cup over?

HIP   H-I-P. HIP. Put your hand on your HIP.

Lesson 15

th th. th says "th," like th-th-thAT.

Tip: Put your tongue on your teeth to say "th".

thAT These letters say "th-A-T." thAT. thAT is my candy.

Note: Lowercase "th" is used to distinguish between its' sound and the T and H sounds.

the These letters say, "th-uh" or "th-ee." The dog is funny.

thIS th-I-S. thIS. Look at thIS mouse.

Lesson 16

R This is the letter R. R says "ur" like r-r-ring.

RAT ur-A-T. RAT. That RAT has a long tail.

RUG ur-uh-G. RUG. Wipe your feet on the RUG please!

RUB ur-uh-B. RUB. Will you RUB my back?

ROB   ur-awe-B. ROB. It is bad to ROB and steal.

RAG   ur-A-G. RAG. I need a RAG to clean the table.

RIP   ur-I-P. RIP. Be careful or you will RIP the pages.

RIB   ur-I-B. RIB. Can you feel your RIB?

TRIP   T-ur-I-P. TRIP. Did the boy TRIP on the ball?

TRAP   T-ur-A-P. TRAP. The man used a TRAP to catch a tiger!

GRAB G-ur-A-B. GRAB. The baby likes to GRAB my hair.

CRIB C-ur-I-B. CRIB. The baby is asleep in a CRIB.

CRAB C-ur-A-B. CRAB. That CRAB pinched me!

BRAG B-ur-A-G. BRAG. It is not nice to BRAG.

Lesson 17

N This is the letter N. N says "N," like n-n-nest.

IN   I-N. IN. Please, come IN the house.

ON   awe-N. ON. Don't jump ON the bed!

PIN   P-I-N. PIN. That PIN and needle both have a sharp point.

PAN   P-A-N. PAN. I used a PAN to cook the pie.

ANT   A-N-T. ANT. The ANT lives in the ground.

RUN   R-uh-N. RUN. Can you RUN fast?

CAN C-A-N. CAN. The soup is in a CAN.

NOT N-O-T. NOT. No, NOT that one.

BUN B-uh-N. BUN. A BUN is a roll of bread.

GUN G-uh-N. GUN. I shot the GUN at a target.

NUT N-U-T. NUT. The squirrel is eating a NUT.

NAP N-A-P. NAP. I feel rested after I take a NAP.

Lesson 18

RUNG ur-uh-N-G. RUNG. A RUNG is a step on a ladder.

HANG H-A-N-G. HANG. HANG your coat up, please.

BANG B-A-N-G. BANG. I love to BANG the drums.

RING ur-I-N-G. RING. Sometimes I wear a RING.

Note: Sometimes "I" makes an "EE" sound.

Lesson 19

S   This is the letter S. S says "S" like s-s-snake.

SIN   S-I-N. SIN. God, please forgive my SIN.

SIT   S-I-T. SIT. Will you SIT in your chair?

SAT   S-A-T. SAT. I SAT on the floor.

BUS   B-uh-S. BUS. Do you take a BUS to school?

SUN S-uh-N. SUN. The SUN is very bright.

GAS G-A-S. GAS. Put GAS in your car to make it go.

PASS P-A-S-S. PASS. We will PASS it.

Note: Two Ss are together, make one S sound.

RUST ur-uh-S-T. RUST. The metal is covered in RUST.

STOP S-T-awe-P. STOP. STOP breaking your toys.

SPIN   S-P-I-N. SPIN. I can SPIN around and around.

SONG   S-O-N-G. SONG. Did you sing a SONG?

SING   S-I-N-G. SING. SING your favorite song.

SANG   S-A-N-G. SANG. I SANG lots of songs at church.

SNIP   S-N-I-P. SNIP. The barber cut a SNIP of my hair.

NAP   N-A-P. NAP. I feel rested after I take a NAP.

SNAP S-N-A-P. SNAP. Can you SNAP your fingers?

STUNT S-T-uh-N-T. STUNT. The acrobat performed a STUNT!

STRING S-T-ur-I-N-G. STRING. A STRING is on your shirt.

STRONG S-T-ur-awe-N-G. STRONG. That man is very STRONG.

Lesson 20

D This is the letter D. D says "D," like d-d-daddy.

DOG D-awe-G. DOG. The DOG won't stop barking.

DIG D-I-G. DIG. Pirates DIG for buried treasure.

HID H-I-D. HID. I HID under my bed.

DOT D-awe-T. DOT. A DOT is a small round mark.

GOD G-awe-D. GOD. GOD is good.

DAD D-A-D. DAD. I love my DAD.

BAD B-A-D. BAD. Were you BAD or good today?

POD P-O-D. POD. The peas are in the POD.

AND A-N-D. AND. I like dogs AND cats.

HAND H-A-N-D. HAND. My HAND has five fingers.

SAND S-A-N-D. SAND. The beach has lots of SAND.

BAND B-A-N-D. BAND. The BAND is playing music.

DRIP D-ur-I-P. DRIP. Did water DRIP on the floor?

DROP D-ur-awe-P. DROP. Don't DROP the baby!

DRAG D-ur-A-G. DRAG. Don't DRAG your blanket!

Lesson 21

E This is the letter E. E says "eh" like e-e-egg.

RED ur-eh-D. RED. My tongue is RED.

HEN H-eh-N. HEN. Our HEN gives us an egg each morning.

PEN P-eh-N. PEN. You can write with a PEN.

TEN T-eh-N. TEN. I can count to TEN!

BED B-eh-D. BED. I like to make my BED.

PET P-eh-T. PET. I PET my dog every day.

NET N-eh-T. NET. I caught a bug in a NET.

RENT ur-eh-N-T. RENT. We will RENT a movie on Friday.

NEST N-eh-S-T. NEST. There are bird eggs in that NEST.

PEST P-eh-S-T. PEST. That grasshopper is a PEST.

BEST B-eh-S-T. BEST. I like ice cream the BEST.

REST ur-eh-S-T. REST. I am tired and need to REST.

Level 2

Once your children have mastered Level 2 Phonics Reading, they will be confident readers. Level 2 starts by introducing simple sentences. At first, you should have your little ones sound out each word individually. However, they will need to reread the sentence over and over again, until they can read it without struggling. Once they can read a sentence with little or no hesitation, you can move to the next sentence.

In the beginning, your progress may be very slow. In fact, you might have to limit yourself to just a few sentences a lesson. The reason is that although your children can read each sentence's individual words, by the time they reach the last word in the sentence, they will have forgotten the first few words.

Do not tolerate guessing. After reading the first few words, many children will simply guess what the rest of the sentence says. To help your children avoid this bad habit, we have excluded pictures and common "logical" sentence structures. We have excluded pictures for the simple reason that we want your children to read, not guess what the sentences say based on the action in pictures.

We have also excluded common or logical sentences. For example, take the sentence "The sky is blue." After reading, "The sky is," a young reader could easily guess that the next word is "blue." To avoid the temptation of guessing, we introduce silly, uncommon, and illogical sentences. These sentences make "guessing" nearly impossible.

You will notice that several letters are italicized. The italicized letters are new sounds for letters that your little ones learned previously. We do not want you to introduce a new "rule" for the italicized letters – at least not yet. Just tell your children that usually the letter says "(whatever the previous rule was)," but sometimes the letter also says, "(whatever the new sound is)."

There are 4 sections in Level 2. The first section is a reading of simple sentences using words from Level 1. The second section transitions from using nearly all capital letters to the proper capitalization for each word. We have repeated all the sentences from section 1, but you will find that the new "properly" capitalized sentences will still take some time for your little ones to recognize.

The third section is "Silly Sentences." In this section, your little ones will get lots of practice reading a variety of sentences. As stated earlier, we used "illogical" sentences so that your children are not tempted to guess what the sentences say, instead of reading the actual words. However, there is also an ulterior motive – silly sentences are fun to read! These sentences make reading just as fun as looking at pictures. So be sure to point out how silly the sentences are after your children read them.

Finally, the last section introduces a host of new sound and letter combinations. Once your children can read all the sentences without hesitation and can recognize the punctuation marks, they are ready to move on.

Lesson 22 (Uppercase Sentences)

GET the BUG.

Note: Sound out each word individually. Then go back and reread the sentence until you can read it without any hesitation.

HOP IN the TUB.

Note: Point to the dot at the end of the sentence. That dot is called a period and it marks the end of a sentence.

thAT PIG IS BIG.

the DOG HAS a BED.

GOD IS STRONG.

the RAT DIGS.

PACK UP the TENT.

Note: Point to the K in the word PACK. That is the letter K, but it makes the same sound as the letter C, k-k-kick.

thIS IS a TEST.

D*O* NOT TRIP ON the BAG.

Note: Point to the "O" in DO. O usually says "awe" like o-o-octopus, but sometimes "O" just says its name, "O".

GRAB the PUP.

the CAT SITS ON *a* RUG.

Note: Point the "A" in CAT and then the "lonely a." Remember "a" usually says "Aaaa," but when "a" is alone it says "A" or "uh."

PICK UP the POT.

the HEN IS IN the NEST.

the BAND SINGS a SONG.

CUT the STRING.

Lesson 23 (Sentence Case)

GET the BUG.

Get the bug.

Note: Read the two sentences above. The sentences look different, but they are the same. There are big and little letters, but they make the same sounds.

*H*op in the tub.

Note: Point to the first letter in this sentence. The first letter in every sentence is BIG, or CAPITAL.

That pig is big.

The dog has a bed.

God is strong.

The rat digs.

Pack up the tent.

This is a test.

Do not trip on the bag.

Don't trip on the BAG.

Note: You can say "do not," or "don't." Just put the words together and replace the "o" in not with an apostrophe.

Grab the pup.

The cat sits on a rug.

Pick up the pot.

The hen is in the nest.

The band sings a song.

Cut the string.

Lesson 24 (Silly Sentences)

Get the strong pig.

That pup is in the tub.

Don't pack up a rat.

Don't hop in the pot.

Did the pick dig?

Note: The mark at the end of this sentence is called a question mark. It means that the sentence is asking a question.

The band sits in a nest.

Sit on the hot hat.

Cut that test up.

Is a hen in that bag?

The rug trips on the dog.

The string has a bed.

The cat sang!

Note: The mark at the end of this sentence is called an "exclamation mark." It means that the sentence is shocking or exciting!

Grab that song!

The gun did not sing.

Did a dog pet the sun?

Did the bus drop a crab?

That bug sat on a rat.

Dad did a big stunt.

That red hog brags.

Take a nap in that tub.

Cats don't sit on ants.

Sand is in this crib!

Bob got a hug.

Not a cop!

Pet the bed.

The ten bags ran.

Lesson 25

F This is the letter F. F says "F," like f-f-fish.

The fig is Fred's.

Fred's raft is fun.

The duck flaps fast.

Is that fig on the fence?

Note: When some letters are together, they make different sounds. Here "ce" makes a "S" sound like "face-ce-ce."

The raft flips on the fence!

ee The double "ee" says its name, "E" like fee-ee-eet – feet.

Note: When some letters are together, they make a different sound.

Get off the free feed.

Is this sticky stuff toffee?

Films keep on the fence.

Is this a free frog?

Get off the fat coffee!

That feed is fast!

Lesson 26

are Note: Don't sound this word out because it is a sight word. Just remember that it says "are," like "Are" you a big kid?

The frog's feet are fat.

Pig and Hen are singing.

Are the pants digging?

L This is the letter L. L says "L," like l-l-lion.

Note: Put the tip of your tongue on the roof of your mouth to make the "l" sound.

That log fell on his leg!

Let's see the little clock.

Let's lock the fence.

Lots of blocks are fun.

Don't get lost, *B*ill.

Note: Point to the capital B in Bill. The first letter in a person's name is BIG, or capital.

Lesson 27

Y This is the letter Y. When y is at the end of a word, it usually says "ee," like Daddy-y-y.

The puppy is happy.

That cat is silly.

This bunny is terribly ill.

Is this free candy sticky?

Isn't that a funny frog?

The little kitty is terrible.

The black egg is sleepy.

M This is the letter M. M says "m," like m-m-monkey.

Note: Be careful not to make an "uh" sound after the M.

The melon is smelly.

My mommy is muddy.

Note: Point to the "Y" in mommy. Y usually says "ee" at the end of a word, but sometimes it says "I," like my-I-I. My.

My feet are very messy.

That man has a mop.

Is this free candy sticky?

Lesson 29

sh Together the letters sh say "sh," like sh-sh-sheep.

Note: When some letters are together, they make a different sound.

Shop at the ring.

She is short and slim.

Note: Point to the "e" in she. E usually says "eh" like e-e-egg, but here it says its name, "EE".

She shot the black ball.

Note: Point to the "a" in ball. "A" usually says "Aaaa," like a-a-apple, but sometimes it says "awe," like in b-awe-awe-awe-ll – ball.

He is not tall.

He runs and falls!

Lesson 30

W This is the letter W. W says "oo," like oo-oo-ooater – water.

Note: Be careful not to make the "uh" sound after the oo.

Will all the fish swim?

We did not need a shell.

What Note: Don't sound this word out because it is a sight word. Just remember that it says "what," like "What are you doing?".

What is he wishing?

Where is that silly list?

Note: Point to the "e" in where. E usually says "eh" like e-e-egg, but here it is silent; it doesn't say anything at all.

Why did he sit?

Lesson 31

V This is the letter V. V says "V," like v-v-vacuum.

We are very wet.

He went **to** the vet.

Note: Point to the "o" in to. O usually says "awe" like o-o-octopus, but sometimes "O" says "oo" like to-oo-oo – to.

Vicky has a penny.

That van is very fast.

Lesson 32

ch Together the letters ch say "ch," like ch-ch-chip.

Note: When some letters are together, they make a different sound.

His chimp wants chicken.

Don't kiss my chilly cheek!

Why is he chatting?

I have cherry on my chin.

Note: Point to the "I". I usually says says "ih" like i-i-insect, but sometimes "I" just says its name, "I."

or Together the letters "or" say "ore" like ore-ore-ornaments.

Note: When some letters are together, they make a different sound.

We have more chores.

Do they have a van or car?

Why are the chips for me?

Did they shut my door?

You Note: Don't sound this word out because it is a sight word. Just remember that it says "you," like You are smart!

You went to lunch.

There you are!

Your shorts are torn.

Wer*e* you at the store?

Note: Point to the "e" in were. E usually says "eh" like e-e-egg, but here it is silent; it doesn't say anything at all.

Lesson 33

 This is the letter X. X says "ks" like si-ks-ks – six.

I can fix that box.

You are visiting a fox.

That's a very strong ox.

J This is the letter J. J says "J," like j-j-jump.

Just jump when you jog!

The red jam is wet.

That junk is very smelly!

The jugs were just filled.

their Note: Don't sound this word out because it is a sight word. Just remember that it says "their," like That is their car.

Their fox is over *there.*

Note: Point to "their" and "there." These words are spelled different and they have different meanings, but they sound the same.

It is their jacket.

Their sheep are all black.

Did you see their ducks?

Lesson 34

Z This is the letter Z. Z says "Z," like z-z-zipper.

Their zebra is not there.

They listen to my jazz.

Note: Point to the double "zz" in the word jazz. There are two Zs, but together they just make one Z sound.

Where is my fuzzy mop?

Zip your zipper!

qu Together the letters "qu" say "koo" like koo-koo-kooick — quick.

Note: When some letters are together, they make a different sound.

The queen just quit!

Their ox is very quick.

What is your question?

She is very qu*i*et.

Note: Point to the "i" in the word quiet. "I" usually says "i" like i-i-insect, but sometimes "I" just says its name, "I."

ay Together the letters "ay" say "A," like way-ay-ay – way.

Note: When some letters are together, they make a different sound.

We can play quietly.

Today, I had a sandwich.

What day in **May** is it?

Note: Point to the "M" in May. The first letter in a name or title is BIG, or capital.

My wheels are gray.

Lesson 36

ai The letters ai usually say "A," like pai-ai-aid – paid.

Note: When some letters are together, they make a different sound.

Her train is on the plain.

Rain, rain, go away!

My feet are in pain.

I will wait for my haircut.

ea Together the letters "ea" say "E," like ea-ea-ear.

Note: When some letters are together, they make a different sound.

Please, eat your peas!

I read books every day.

Did you heat up the ham?

Where is your ear?

Lesson 37

ir The letters ir say "ur," like bur-ur-urd – bird.

That girl has a green bird.

She has a very long skirt.

Do not eat the dirt!

His shirt is gray.

oa These letters say "O," like oa-oa-oatmeal.

The goat can lift a load.

No, don't eat their soap!

Why is my boat in the road?

Please, get my toast.

ur The letters ur say "ur," like pur-ur-urse – purse.

I go to church on Sunday.

We didn't burn their toast.

My teacher has a hurt bird.

Purple squirrels are silly.

Lesson 38

our Note: Don't sound this word out because it is a sight word. Just remember that it says "our," like "Our house is nice."

Our chores are so fun.

those Note: Don't sound this word out because it is a sight word. Just remember that it says "those," like "Those are my kittens."

Those are not ours.

Are those pants yours or ours?

Our job is to get the gold.

Note: Point to the "o" in the word gold. O usually says "awe" like o-o-octopus, but sometimes "O" just says its name, "O."

ew The letters ew usually say "oo," like blew-ew-ew – blew.

Their new bird is a duck.

Few eat their feed.

Lesson 39

gh The letters gh sometimes say "f," like rouf-f-f – rough.

Did he just laugh at us?

Their few oxen are tough.

"Enough is enough," I say.

er The letters er usually say "ur," like buttur-ur-ur – butter.

My herd is very big!

Are mermaids in the sea?

Lesson 40

I will g**o** over there.

Note: Point to the "o" in the word go. O usually says "awe" like o-o-octopus, but sometimes "O" just says its name, "O."

Did Dad say no?

That doll is so big!

oo The letters "oo" usually say "ouh," like l-ouh-k – look.

Look, Daddy took the hook.

He is kicking his foot.

Did you look at the frog?

I will cook the corn.

Lesson 41

ue The letters "ue" say "ew," like trew-ew-ew – true.

Don't step on the glue.

Is the ball blue or red?

That is not true!

Lesson 42

oy The letters "oy" say "oy," like toy-oy-oy – toy.

Is he a boy or a man?

This is a silly toy.

God is my great joy.

The queen has a royal bird.

love Note: Don't sound this word out because it is a sight word. Just remember that it says "love," like "I love you."

I love God very much.

He loves to look at doves.

Note: Love is a sight word, but the combination of "ove" is heard in many other words. Point to the "ove" in doves.

Do you love blue or black?

She loves her new gloves.

Lesson 43

aw These letters say "aw," like saw-aw-aw – saw.

Do you love all hawks?

I just saw the queen!

He draws on the lawn.

Look at the little fawn.

Lesson 44

OW The letters "ow" say "O," like
ro-o-o – row.

They row so slow.

Do not throw pink snow!

Hawks are faster than crows.

Look at that corn grow.

Lesson 45

wr The letters "wr" say "r," like wr-r-rong – wrong.

He will break his wrist!

Please, wrap this gift.

You are wrong!

She wrecked her car!

Level 3

This book is the third and final book in Blue Manor's phonics series. Phonics 3 begins by teaching children that not all letters, especially the vowels, make the same sounds when they appear in different words.

Although vowels can make different sounds, the process is not completely random. Vowels make certain sounds based on the other vowels and consonants that they are paired with. The next section uses rhyming words to show children the different vowel sounds.

The final section introduces children to silent letters. Certain letters remain silent when paired with other letters. The silent letter section helps children recognize when and which letters are silent.

Once your children can read all the words and sentences without hesitation, you can consider them competent readers.

Lesson 46 (Vowels)

a, e, i, o, u
and sometimes
y.

Note: The letters above are vowels. Vowels make different sounds in different words. There are only 5 proper vowels, but 15 vowel sounds.

a
can say...

"aaa" as in cat.

"A" as in cake.

"ah" as in father.

e can say...	"eh" as in egg. "E" as in eat.

i can say...	"i" as in sit. "I" as in bike.

o can say...	"aw" as in lot. "O" as in broke. "uh" as in done.

u can say...	"uh" as in up. "U" as in unicorn.

y
can say...

"y" as in you.

"I" as in why.

"ih" as in myth.

Lesson 47 (Rhyming Words)

Rhyme: Cat, Rat

Note: Listen to the words cat and rat. Don't they sound similar? That is because they are rhyming words. When two words each end in a syllable that sounds similar to the other word, it is called a rhyme.

Read the words that Rhyme with:

at

bat, brat, cat, chat, fat, hat, mat, pat, rat, sat, spat, splat, tat, that, vat.

Read the sentences with:

at

Note: Read the sentences below. See if you can identify the rhyming "at" words.

That brat hurt my cat!

The fat rat just ran.

Please, don't pat my hat.

I wanted to chat; he only sat.

Look at that under the mat!

Lesson 48

Read the words that Rhyme with:

ail

fail, frail, hail, jail, mail, nail, pail, rail, sail, snail, tail, trail.

Read the sentences with:

ail

That snail has a slimy tail!

I followed the trail into jail!

Is there any mail in that pail?

Careful for the nail in the rail.

After a storm, my sail is frail.

Lesson 49

Read the words that Rhyme with:

ain

brain, chain, drain, gain, grain, main, pain, plain, rain, slain, stain, strain, train.

Read the sentences with:

ain

Did the rain stain your shirt?

There is a strain on my brain.

The main chain is on the train.

We gathered grain on the plain.

Our gain went down the drain.

Lesson 50

Read the words that Rhyme with:

ake

bake, cake, fake, flake, make, lake, quake, rake, sake, stake, take, wake.

Read the sentences with:

ake

You need flour to bake a cake.

Did you take my snow flake?

Let's make a rake for fun.

That lake isn't real; it is fake.

For my sake, use the stake.

Lesson 51

Read the words that Rhyme with:

ad

bad, brad, dad, fad, glad, had, lad, mad, pad, rad, sad, tad.

Read the sentences with:

ad

He is not sad; he is glad.

That is the lad of that dad.

I think that he is a tad mad.

I had a brad, but lost it.

It is a fad to kick the pad.

Lesson 52

Read the words that Rhyme with:

ale

bale, gale, kale, male, pale, sale, scale, tale, whale.

Read the sentences with:

ale

Can you put a whale on a scale?

The pale dog was a male.

He told a tale about a gale.

Please put the bale on sale.

The big whale ate kale.

Lesson 53

Read the words that Rhyme with:

all

ball, call, fall, hall, mall, small, tall, wall.

Read the sentences with:

all

The hall has a very thick wall.

I call the ball!

It was a very small mall.

I feel tall in the fall.

Did you call the mall yet?

Lesson 54

Read the words that Rhyme with:

ame

blame, came, fame, flame, frame, game, lame, name, same, shame, tame.

Read the sentences with:

ame

Don't play the blame game!

It's a shame, the lion isn't tame.

What a small and lame flame.

His name has great fame.

No, it's not the same frame.

Lesson 55

Read the words that Rhyme with:

an

ban, can, clan, fan, man, pan, plan, ran, scan, tan, van.

Read the sentences with:

an

They had to ban that crazy fan.

That man ran as fast as a van.

A clan has more than one man.

She put the can in the pan.

My plan was to pass the scan.

Lesson 56

Read the words that Rhyme with:

ank

bank, blank, crank, drank, plank, sank, spank, tank, thank, yank.

Read the sentences with:

ank

He walked the plank and sank.

A tank ran over the bank.

Thank you, I drank it.

Don't yank the crank too hard.

The bank sign was blank.

Lesson 57

Read the words that Rhyme with:

ap

cap, clap, flap, gap, lap, map, nap, rap, sap, scrap, slap, snap, tap, trap.

Read the sentences with:

ap

Don't tap, clap!

Did the trap snap shut?

The map is hidden in his cap.

My cat took a nap in mom's lap.

Just scrap that old flap.

Lesson 58

Read the words that Rhyme with:

ar

bar, char, car, far, jar, mar, par, scar, spar, tar, star.

Read the sentences with:

ar

Did the fire char our jar?

That hot tar will mar the house.

It's her scar from the car crash.

We often spar with a bar.

I hit the ball far and got a par.

Lesson 59

Read the words that Rhyme with:

ash

bash, cash, crash, dash, flash, gash, hash, mash, rash, sash, slash, smash, splash, trash.

Read the sentences with:

ash

Did he mash the trash?

Don't flash the cash.

There was a dash and a crash!

Her sash gave her a rash.

The bash made a huge gash.

Lesson 60

Read the words that Rhyme with:

ack

back, black, crack, clack, jack, lack, pack, quack, rack, sack, slack, snack, stack, tack, track.

Read the sentences with:

ack

The pack and sack were black.

Don't stack the pack on a rack.

There is a crack on the track.

Eat those stacks of snacks.

Is there a tack in your back?

Lesson 61

Read the words that Rhyme with:

aw

claw, draw, flaw, jaw, law, paw, saw, straw, thaw.

Read the sentences with:

aw

There is a big claw in that paw.

The cow had straw in her jaw.

Only I saw the flaw in his work.

Did you draw what you saw?

It can't thaw; it is the law.

Lesson 62

Read the words that Rhyme with:

ay

bay, clay, day, gay, gray, hay, lay, may, okay, pay, play, spray, stay, tray, way.

Read the sentences with:

ay

The cow lay down in the hay.

Okay, I'd love to play.

You should stay near the bay.

Did he pay for that tray of food?

I will lead the way all day!

Lesson 63

Read the words that Rhyme with:

eal

appeal, conceal, deal, heal, ideal, meal, peal, real, seal, steal, teal, veal.

Read the sentences with:

eal

Did the lion conceal his meal?

I think that the seal will heal.

It would be ideal, if it was real.

Veal was his meal.

If you did not steal, appeal!

116

Lesson 64

Read the words that Rhyme with:

ear

appear, clear, dear, fear, gear, hear, near, rear, tear.

Read the sentences with:

ear

Dear, did you clear the table?

It does appear to be very near.

I fear that I don't have the gear.

Is it near the rear?

Can you hear without the gear?

Lesson 65

Read the words that Rhyme with:

eat

beat, cheat, feat, heat, meat, neat, pleat, seat, treat, wheat.

Read the sentences with:

eat

What a great feat, for that treat!

Isn't that a neat seat?

Do you like meat or wheat?

That is your seat in the heat.

If you cheat, you will be beat!

118

Lesson 66

Read the words that Rhyme with:

eed

bleed, breed, creed, deed, feed, need, seed, speed, steed, weed.

Read the sentences with:

eed

That dog breed loves to feed.

That weed made me bleed.

We have a need for a creed.

The steed ran at a high speed.

Is free seed part of his deed?

Lesson 67

Read the words that Rhyme with:

eel

feel, heel, peel, reel, steel, wheel.

Read the sentences with:

eel

How does your heel feel?

That reel is made of steel.

Peel the sticker off the wheel.

Your heel is on my reel.

Do you feel the steel?

Lesson 68

Read the words that Rhyme with:

eep

beep, creep, deep, keep, peep, seep, sheep, sleep, steep, sweep, weep.

Read the sentences with:

eep

If you can't sleep, count sheep.

Did the slime seep deep?

The sheep peep at the dogs.

Is that a beep or a weep?

Sweep the steep path.

Lesson 69

Read the words that Rhyme with:

eet

beet, greet, meet, sheet, street.

Read the sentences with:

eet

Greet him when you meet him.

Did you greet him on the street?

There is a beet in this sheet.

Are your feet in the street?

The ships meet the other fleet.

Lesson 70

ell

bell, cell, dwell, fell, hell, shell, smell, spell, swell, tell, well, yell.

Read the sentences with:

ell

Please don't yell, just tell.

Can you smell this shell?

The prisoners dwell in a cell.

Yes, he fell in a deep well!

Can you spell swell?

Lesson 71

Read the words that Rhyme with:

en

amen, den, hen, men, pen, ten, then, when, wren.

Read the sentences with:

en

The men are in the den.

That hen lives in the pen.

If not then, when?

With a pen he wrote "amen."

That's a wren, not a hen.

Lesson 72

Read the words that Rhyme with:

ent

bent, cent, dent, event, lent, scent, sent, spent, went.

Read the sentences with:

ent

He spent every cent!

A scent sent the dog running.

Yes, we went to the event.

A car was bent and had a dent.

She only lent me a cent.

Lesson 73

Read the words that Rhyme with:

est

best, crest, chest, guest, lest, nest, pest, rest, test, vest, west, zest.

Read the sentences with:

est

The poor guest got no rest.

The vest covered his chest.

Do your best and pass the test.

I told the pest to head west.

A nest was on the hill's crest.

Lesson 74

Read the words that Rhyme with:

ew

chew, crew, dew, few, grew, Jew, new, knew, pew, screw, shrew, stew, threw, view.

Read the sentences with:

ew

Do not chew on your stew.

The tiny shrew drank the dew.

His crew threw the door open.

I knew that the car wasn't new.

Few have such a nice view.

Lesson 75

ice

advice, dice, lice, mice, nice, price, rice, slice, spice, twice, vice.

Read the sentences with:

ice

Those mice eat the rice.

What is the price per slice?

Look twice for head lice!

That is very nice advice.

Playing dice can be a vice.

Lesson 76

Read the words that Rhyme with:

ick

brick, chick, click, flick, kick, lick, pick, quick, sick, slick, stick, thick, trick, tick, wick.

Read the sentences with:

ick

Don't kick that brick!

Give that tick a flick!

That little chick looks sick.

Did you pick the candle wick?

That stick is too thick.

Lesson 77

id

did, forbid, grid, hid, kid, lid, rid, slid, squid.

Read the sentences with:

id

I forbid the kid to go!

Did you try the squid?

Please don't get rid of the lid.

The rat hid in that grid.

A kid slid in the mud.

Lesson 78

Read the words that Rhyme with:

ide

bride, decide, glide, guide, hide, pride, ride, side, slide, stride, tide, wide.

Read the sentences with:

ide

The bride was by his side.

Do you need a guide to decide?

I have too much pride to hide.

I moved with a glide and a slide.

Did you slide on the ride?

Lesson 79

ight

bright,   flight,   fight,   fright, height,   light,   might,   night, right, sight, slight, tight.

Read the sentences with:

ight

It was not a bright light.

Fight with all your might!

There is little sight at night.

The flight belts were tight.

His big height caused a fright.

Lesson 80

Read the words that Rhyme with:
ile

bile, exile, file, mile, pile, rile, smile, tile, vile, while.

Read the sentences with:
ile

Moses spent a while in exile.

The pile was sitting on the tile.

I try to smile every mile.

The green bile was vile.

That file sure did rile her.

Lesson 81

Read the words that Rhyme with:

ill

chill, dill, drill, grill, hill, kill, mill, pill, sill, skill, spill, still, thrill, will.

Read the sentences with:

ill

The dark mill gave me a chill.

Careful, that pill will kill.

His will was with the drill.

The gill is on top of the hill.

Those with skill don't spill.

Lesson 82

Read the words that Rhyme with:

in

begin, bin, chin, fin, grin, pin, shin, sin, skin, spin, thin, tin, twin, win.

Read the sentences with:

in

Do not even begin to sin.

I scraped the skin on my shin.

The bin was made of tin.

She wore a grin above her chin.

Her twin was very thin.

Lesson 83

Read the words that Rhyme with:

ind

bind, blind, find, grind, kind, mind, rind, wind.

Read the sentences with:

ind

The blind man was very kind.

I used my mind to find the gold.

Wind the cord to bind it.

Did you grind the melon's rind?

The blind can still find things.

Lesson 84

Read the words that Rhyme with:

ine

dine, fine, line, mine, nine,
pine, shine, spine, vine, wine.

Read the sentences with:

ine

Grapes off the vine make wine.

Gold in a mine will shine.

I counted nine pine trees.

That spot in line is mine!

Does your spine feel fine?

Lesson 85

Read the words that Rhyme with:

ing

bring, cling, fling, king, ping, ring, sing, spring, sting, string, swing, thing.

Read the sentences with:

ing

Did the groom bring the ring?

The king loves to sing.

Please don't swing that string!

What did you bring this spring?

Don't you cling to that thing!

Lesson 86

Read the words that Rhyme with:

ink

blink, drink, link, pink, rink, shrink, sink, stink, think, wink.

Read the sentences with:

ink

I think that I smell stink.

Do you drink pink soda?

Was that a blink or a wink?

Did the ice rink shrink?

Link the sink to the tub.

Lesson 87

Read the words that Rhyme with:

ip

chip, clip, dip, drip, flip, grip, hip, rip, ship, sip, skip, slip, tip, trip, whip.

Read the sentences with:

ip

Don't slip or you'll chip a tooth!

Did you just skip or trip?

I saw the tip of the whip rip it!

Get a grip or you will flip!

I love to dip my chip in salsa.

Lesson 88

Read the words that Rhyme with:

it

bit, fit, hit, kit, knit, lit, pit,
quit, sit, skit, spit, split, wit.

Read the sentences with:

it

I like to sit when I knit.

He spit into the deep pit.

Use your wit and don't quit.

He threw a fit and hit me!

Let's split this kit.

Lesson 89

Read the words that Rhyme with:

oat

boat, coat, float, oat, throat.

Read the sentences with:

oat

Will this boat float?

Take this to coat your throat.

I left my coat on the boat!

The oat was stuck in her throat.

Why didn't the coat float?

Lesson 90

Read the words that Rhyme with:

ock

block, clock, dock, flock, knock, lock, mock, rock, shock, sock.

Read the sentences with:

ock

Did you just mock my sock?

I was in shock to see the clock.

Please don't rock the dock.

Did you lock up your flock?

You saw him knock the block.

Lesson 91

og

bog, dog, fog, frog, hog, jog, log,   smog.

Read the sentences with:

og

My hog is lost in the fog.

There is a frog on that log!

I took my dog for a jog.

There was a log in the bog.

That isn't fog; it's smog!

Lesson 92

Read the words that Rhyme with:

oil

boil, broil, foil, soil, spoil, toil.

Read the sentences with:

oil

I love to toil in the soil.

Put it in tin foil or it will spoil.

Do I boil or broil the meat?

Can soil ever spoil?

Did you boil the egg in tin foil?

Lesson 93

Read the words that Rhyme with:

old

bold, cold, fold, gold, hold, mold, scold, sold, told.

Read the sentences with:

old

He sold all of his gold.

I told you it was cold.

Did she hold the mold?

He is bold to scold that man.

Will you hold this fold?

146

Lesson 94

Read the words that Rhyme with:

oke

broke, choke, coke, joke, poke, smoke, spoke, stroke, woke.

Read the sentences with:

oke

Did she choke on that coke?

He woke from the poke.

A stroke is not a joke!

She spoke standing in smoke.

It broke the smoke alarm!

Lesson 95

ook

book,   brook,   cook,   crook,

hook, look, nook, shook, took.

Read the sentences with:

ook

She took my book.

Did you look at that hook?

Look for the crook!

I cook the fish from the brook.

Look for a book in that nook.

148

Lesson 96

Read the words that Rhyme with:

ool

cool, drool, fool, pool, school, stool, tool.

Read the sentences with:

ool

Do not drool in the pool!

He was a fool in school.

Stand on a stool to get the tool.

The pool was nice and cool.

I left the tool at the school.

Lesson 97

oom

boom, bloom, broom, doom, gloom, loom, room, zoom.

Read the sentences with:

oom

Use a broom to clean a room.

It is not all doom and gloom.

Did a flower bloom on the loom?

Don't zoom into the room!

A boom made my broom drop.

Lesson 98

Read the words that Rhyme with:

op

bop, chop, cop, crop, drop, flop, hop, mop, shop, slop, stop, top.

Read the sentences with:

op

Can you mop the shop?

I saw the cop hop over a fence.

Go to the top shop.

I flop slop in the pig's pen.

The wind made the crop drop.

Lesson 99

Read the words that Rhyme with:

ore

bore, chore, core, more, score, shore, snore, sore, store, tore, wore.

Read the sentences with:

ore

We have to score more to win!

Sadly, I tore the dress I wore.

A sore bore down into his skin.

Owning a store is a big chore.

I found this core on the shore.

Lesson 100

Read the words that Rhyme with:

orn

born, corn, forlorn, horn, scorn, thorn, torn.

Read the sentences with:

orn

Her sheet was torn by a thorn.

She was born to eat corn.

I felt forlorn from their scorn.

Was I cut by a thorn or a horn?

The forlorn man ate some corn.

Lesson 101

Read the words that Rhyme with:

ost

post, ghost, host, most, post.

Note: In some words, the "o" in ost makes the long "O" sound.

Read the sentences with:

ost

I like this host the most.

The ghost was not a good host.

I sent the post to the host.

Which ghost do you like most?

That post was the most liked.

Lesson 102

Read the words that Rhyme with:

ost

cost, frost, lost.

Note: In some words, the "o" in ost makes the short O sound "ah."

Read the sentences with:

ost

He paid a cost to save the lost.

The lost are covered in frost.

What is the cost to defrost it?

The frost will cost us our crop.

Lesson 103

Read the words that Rhyme with:

ot

blot, cot, clot, got, jot, hot, knot, lot, not, plot, pot, rot, shot, spot, tot, trot.

Read the sentences with:

ot

I slept on a cot on a hot day.

I got a knot in my hair!

This is not the spot.

That is a lot of shot.

Did the food in the pot rot?

Lesson 104

Read the words that Rhyme with:

ought

bought,   brought,   fought, sought, thought.

Read the sentences with:

ought

He brought all that he bought.

He fought for what he sought.

I thought that I brought it!

She bought into the thought.

Lesson 105

Read the words that Rhyme with:

ow

cow, bow, brow, how, now, plow, wow.

Read the sentences with:

ow

The silly cow took a bow.

Can you plow the field now?

Let the cow pull the plow.

Wow, that is a nice brow.

How do you bow down so far?

Lesson 106

Read the words that Rhyme with: *ow*

blow, bow, crow, flow, glow, grow, know, row, show, slow, snow, throw.

Note: In some words, the "o" in ow makes the long "O" sound.

Read the sentences with: *ow*

How the snow did blow.

You don't throw the bow.

That crow sure did grow.

I know a good show to watch.

The flow was very slow.

Read the words that Rhyme with:

own

crown, brown, clown, down, drown, gown, town.

Read the sentences with:

own

Please don't drown the clown!

She wore her gown into town.

The king threw his crown down.

Her gown was all brown.

Will he drown down there?

Lesson 108

Read the words that Rhyme with:

ump

bump, clump, dump, hump, jump, lump, plump, pump, rump, slump, stump, thump.

Read the sentences with:

ump

Is it a hump or a bump?

That hippo has a plump rump.

Use a pump to dump the water.

Try to jump over the stump!

Don't slump on the pump.

Lesson 109

Read the words that Rhyme with:

unk

bunk, chunk, clunk, drunk, dunk, flunk, hunk, junk, punk, shrunk, skunk, sunk.

Read the sentences with:

unk

That skunk stunk really bad!

It is nothing but a hunk of junk.

Did the punk flunk out?

The chunk sunk into the mud.

The hunk of fruit shrunk.

Lesson 110

Read the words that Rhyme with:

uck

buck, chuck, cluck, duck, luck, pluck, puck, struck, stuck, suck, truck, tuck.

Read the sentences with:

uck

A buck was stuck in the muck.

Did you pluck that duck?

It was luck that saved the truck.

He struck the hockey puck.

I heard a stuck chicken cluck.

Lesson 111

Read the words that Rhyme with:

ug

bug, chug, drug, dug, jug, lug, mug, plug, rug, shrug, slug, snug.

Read the sentences with:

ug

I saw the bug shrug.

A slug slid into the mug.

Put the plug in the jug.

Did you lug the rug in there?

The rat dug into a snug hole.

Lesson 112

Read the words that Rhyme with:

y

cry, dry, fly, fry, guy, my, shy, sky, sly, spy, try, why.

Read the sentences with:

y

I had to dry my shirt.

That spy is really sly.

Why is the pretty girl shy?

I will try to catch the fly.

The guy likes to fry chicken.

Lesson 113 (Silent Letters)

Read the words with a silent letter: *ch*

ache, anchor, character, choir, chord, Christian, Christmas, echo, orchid, school.

Note: Sometimes when c and h are together, the (h) is silent; only the (c) makes a sound.

Read the sentences with a silent letter: *ch*

The Christian has character.

A chord held the anchor.

I heard an echo in the school.

I love the Christmas choir!

I grew an orchid for Christmas.

Lesson 114

Read the words with a silent letter: *gn*

align, design, gnarl, gnat, sign.

Note: When g and n are together, the (g) is silent; only the (n) makes a sound.

Read the sentences with a silent letter: *gn*

I love that design.

Did you align the books?

It is not a fly; it's a tiny gnat.

Could you read that sign?

What a big gnarl on that tree.

Lesson 115

Read the words with a silent letter: *kn*

knee, knew, knife, knight, knit, knot, know, knuckle.

Note: When k and n are together, the (k) is silent; only the (n) makes a sound.

Read the sentences with a silent letter: *kn*

I knew he was a singer.

Did you knit that sweater?

The knight had a knife.

I know how to tie a knot.

It hit her knee, not her knuckle.

Lesson 116

Read the words with a silent letter: **mb**

bomb, climb, comb, crumb, dumb, lamb, numb, thumb.

Note: When m and b are together, the (b) is silent; only the (m) makes a sound.

Read the sentences with a silent letter: **mb**

Was that a bomb?

How high can you climb?

The lamb ate the crumb.

My thumb is numb.

Don't forget to comb your hair.

Lesson 117

Read the words with a silent letter: *SC*

ascend, scene, scent.

Note: When s and c are together, the (c) is silent; only the (s) makes a sound.

Read the sentences with a silent letter: *SC*

Jesus did ascend into Heaven.

What scene are you acting?

The hound dog had the scent.

Please stop creating a scene!

Do you smell a scent in the air?

Lesson 118

Read the words with a silent letter: **st**

apostle, hustle, bristle, thistle, wrestle.

Note: Sometimes when s and t are together, the (t) is silent; only the (s) makes a sound.

Read the sentences with a silent letter: **st**

Paul was an Apostle of Christ.

Those boys love to wrestle.

Can you hustle inside, please?

The thistle poked my hand!

The angry dog's fur bristled.

Lesson 119

Read the words with a silent letter: *ui*

biscuit, built, circuit, guilt, guitar.

Note: Sometimes when u and i are together, the (u) is silent; only the (i) makes a sound.

Read the sentences with a silent letter: *ui*

The girl ate the biscuit.

The man was full of guilt.

Noah built a great ark.

That cowboy plays guitar.

Did he replace a circuit board?

Lesson 120

Read the words with a silent letter: _wr_

wrap, wreck, wren, wrench, wring, wrist, write, wrong, wrote.

Note: When w and r are together, the (w) is silent; only the (r) makes a sound.

Read the sentences with a silent letter: _wr_

Turn the wrench right.

Did you like writing that song?

A wren sung a beautiful song.

You will wreck the ship!

How did you hurt your wrist?

173

Congratulations!
You are an early-reader!

Made in the USA
Charleston, SC
27 December 2016